THE AUTHENTIC
BOOK OF POEMS

SHAKIRA HENDERSON

The Authentic Book of Poems

By
Shakira Henderson

Published by
Meet the World Image Solutions

www.mtwimagesolutions.com

Copyright © 2024
Shakira Henderson

Cover design by Dr. Rhonda M. Lawson

ISBN: 979-8-9872429-4-0
Meet the World Image Solutions

Dedication

In loving memory of my mother, Renocka, who is the prettiest star in the sky. May these tales reach you. Your legacy will always live on through me. To my father, James, a hero walking alongside me, often unnoticed. My brothers, Clancy, Jimmie, Ojai, and James, who saw potential in me and fanned the spark into a flame. To my daughter, Zyonah, my love, my life, my light. For my daycare kids, whose laughter is my favorite sound. For every reader who finds pieces of themselves within these pages. Thank you for giving my voice a chance and making this journey worthwhile.

Acknowledgments

"It is absolutely terrifying the kind of deep suffering the happiest looking people are able to hide inside themselves."

- Nikita Gill

I would like to acknowledge every young person who has suffered in silence, who has grown physically, but struggled emotionally, spiritually, and mentally. Those who have found creative ways to use their gifts and talents to create utterances of their welfare. To those who are in leadership, dedicating themselves to providing safe spaces for individuals who have suffered in silence to be seen, heard, and valued, thank you for being a light in dark places.

"God is the one who gives seed to those who plant."

- 2 Corinthians 9:6

I want to thank Dr. Roxie Dennis and Laponda Palmer for trusting the God in them to plant spiritual seeds in me as a child. Out of your obedience, I have a "nothing can separate me from God's love" type of approach! If it weren't for the spiritual foundation, I don't know how I would have been able to do this thing called life.

I would like to acknowledge Chereé Robinson for believing in the journey God has me on and introducing me to my publisher/editor. Thank you, Chereé, for your love and support. To my publisher and editor Rhonda Lawson, thank you for your expertise, devotion and guidance on this book. Your remarkable brilliance and the endless amount of time and effort that you put forth in bringing my vision into manifestation is immeasurable.

I would love to thank my village of accountability partners and intercessors for keeping me grounded and covered: Jeremy Dix, Melissa

Smith and family, Danisha Tate and family, Julius Wilkerson, Shinelle Sadberry and family, Vondesha King, Lashaun Pearson, Lyndsay Jackson and family, and the Well Church Family. To my therapist, Meg Cohen, for acknowledging "I am not a product of my circumstances, but a product of my decisions."

To the organizations God allowed me to shepherd, Women Empowering Other Women and Let's Talk Empowerment, thank you for trusting me to teach, offering a safe place to be vulnerable and helping you to discover more about yourself.

I want to thank God for anyone who ever lost me in the phases of life. Thank you for giving me that time and space for God to truly develop me into the woman I am today. Lastly, I would like to thank God for creating, shaping, and continually molding me and the gifts that are inside of me. Without God, I would be nothing. Everything that I went through was for His glory and for my better good.

Contents

Encouragement — 71

Introduction

For as long as I can remember, I have always been intuitive. I could always feel when someone wasn't authentic around me, or the Divine would reveal it to me in a dream or vision. This led me to disconnect from people, places, and things that didn't serve me.

Although this is ideal for some, it often left me feeling unworthy, unwanted, and lonely, until God gave me a different revelation. The Divine showed me that I was a leader. I was a visionary. I was unique. Yet, in different seasons of my life, I felt it was untrue due to my experiences and challenges. I experienced molestation, incest, and suicide at a very young age. I also had a learning disability. On top of that, I went through heartbreak and disappointment in my teenage years, which led me to become a single mother. Even in my adult years, I endured rape, grief, and purlion.

Enduring all of those things swallowed my voice, but it led me to write. It was hard for me to confront issues, so instead, I would just write about them. Journaling and writing poems became my savior. One day, God woke me up and spoke *Authentic Book of Poems*.

I discovered that letting someone go due to their lack of self-accountability doesn't exempt me from the pain they caused while in my presence. Instead of just walking away from those individuals, I also NEEDED to confront them. There isn't enough discussion on grieving individuals who are still physically here. You have no idea how many times I wrote and rehearsed what I would say to a person. I don't deem myself a confrontational person, so this was a challenge. I had to choose myself because the little girl inside me was crying. I wouldn't speak up for her then. Now that I'm fully aware of what could have taken my voice, I still sometimes have trouble speaking up for that little girl in me, but it has become easier.

I know it can be difficult. but choose *you* every time. I know you've heard this a million times, BUT CHOOSE YOU EVERY TIME!

Be your authentic self, like I'm learning to do. Don't allow your situation and circumstances to victimize you. Don't beg anyone who doesn't serve you good fruit to stay in your presence. Validate yourself and give them a *no, thank you.*

My goal in writing *The Authentic Book of Poems* is to reach my village. I want to reach humans all over who lost their voices due to their trauma and challenges. Understand you are never alone. Someone out there needs you to survive. Don't be ashamed of your story. It's a great testament to how God can allow you to endure all of what you have been through and still see your sparkle on earth.

Inside, you will find some of my poems and writing prompts to help you identify areas of your life that should be celebrated, or areas of improvement. These prompts may trigger unhealed wounds. It did for me, which made me seek professional therapeutic help. If this triggers you in any way, I recommend getting some type of help, whatever and however that may look for you, as long as it is healthy. It is okay to seek help.

I hope this reaches my village in such an impactful way that they no longer leave their voices, gifts, and boundaries dormant.

With love,
Shakira

Journey to Self-Reflection

Truth

I know where my truth lies.
Vindictive, the enemy is,
To confuse
Strength and vulnerability
As if you have to have one
Without the other.
When my strength arises,
It arises in the comfort
Of my authentic self,
So why deny,
Hide,
Or compromise
My cry for help?
Why be ashamed
Of vulnerability
When God gave you those emotions
To channel through
Giving you possibilities
Of the ability
To see, feel, and sense things
On a deeper, passionate focal view?
It's okay to be overwhelmed
With the waves of life crashing.
Being mad or unhappy,
It's tough,
But understand
And know
Life is about a journey.
There will be ups,

There will be downs.
Just know,
Even in your emotions,
You can always
Still wear your crown.
You're beautiful, Queen.
Even in the silence of your storms,
Your tears are made loud.
As the writer once wrote,
In a full heart, there's room for everything,
And in a heart that's empty, there's room for nothing.

Writing Prompt: What was something you thought was a weakness about yourself, but God showed you it was a strength?

_____

_____

_____

_____

_____

_____

_____

_____

_____

_____

_____

_____

_____

_____

_____

_____

_____

_____

_____

_____

_____

_____

_____

_____

_____

The Call

I didn't ask for this.
My call,
That is.
The call is sacred.
You can be in a room
Full of people
And feel the
Empty hearts there.
Not everyone
Can handle it—
Praying,
Up all night,
Fasting, waiting, working
While believing
That everything,
One day,
Will be alright.
Why He trusts me,
I don't know,
But I have an idea, though:
Maybe
It's because
I carry myself
With value,
Even though,
Deep down inside,
I feel like
I'm hiding,
Drowning

In an ocean
Of ideas.
Overthinking thoughts,
Replaying every promise,
He spoke.

People around me
Sleeping
While I'm
Woke.
Maybe
It's because
I don't care
What they say
Or do anymore
Because I'm hip
To the games
They try to play to score,
Or,
Is it, Lord,
That I'm tired
Of seeing our sisters
Clown one another,
Jealous and envious
Of each other.
I am
My sister's keeper!
Yes, I am
Your loudest cheerleader!
Baby feeding,
Graduation,
Promotions,
And—yes, sis—

I'm definitely
Cheering for that ring
He bought you!
I'm the sister
I never got to meet.
I'm a mother,
A teacher,
With a child
Struggling to read.
Running around town
To different cities,
Feeling defeated
Because it's my own child
Who I can't reach.
The enemy tried
To bottle me up
With guilt
Because her daddy
Claimed he loved me,
And left me young with a baby.
I had no clue
As to
What I was to do.
See, I was just a kid, myself,
Acting like a lady,
Growing up
Beyond my years
Because it was my mistakes
That made me.
I asked many times
For God
To take this cup away from me,
But the more I asked,

The more I bleed.
I know God
Has a purpose,
And I know
God has a plan,
But it doesn't make me exempt
From humiliation,
Prosecution,
Loneliness.
I get that
Whatever life brings me,
I know
I'll have a tribe of women
Standing
Alongside me,
Pursing,
Viewing,
And honoring themselves.
My call isn't just
About me.
I am
My sister's keeper,
So when she cries,
I cry.
The world
Begins weeping
For the power
They failed
To see
In our Black Queens.
We are so needed.

Writing Prompt: What do you believe to be your calling on this earth?

_____

_____

_____

_____

_____

_____

_____

_____

_____

_____

_____

_____

_____

_____

_____

_____

_____

_____

_____

_____

_____

_____

_____

_____

_____

Ascension

This is me daily.
The world
Labeled me
With these names,
And one listed
Crazy.

I'm sure of myself.
Climbing out of the darkness
Looking for help,
But no one is there.

No one knows
The places I've been,
And what I've been shown
During those times I cried out to God.
He allowed me to know
This place that I was in
Was what was required
To reach my next level.

I would have to trust God
And remain positive.
I would have to pick up a pen
And journal
If I needed to vent.
No one would understand
This place I was called to be in.

If only they understood
It's a higher calling
When it's all bad,
But God
Is still good.

Writing Prompt: How important is it to you to evolve in God?

_____
_____
_____
_____
_____
_____
_____
_____
_____
_____
_____
_____
_____
_____
_____
_____
_____
_____
_____
_____
_____
_____
_____
_____
_____
_____
_____
_____
_____

Who is She?

Who am I?
I am she.
Born with a gift
to give the nations.
Like a mermaid who swam
across the sea,
running from plantation to plantation
from slave masters
who tried to kill me.
Like a unicorn,
different and unique,
not in competition
with anyone,
my beauty lies within
just me.
A mother of many,
planting seeds,
producing sprouts,
connected with her inner-most being.
No attention-seeking
or attitude-wearing here.
{a hair flip insert there}
I'm the woman
I'm desiring to be,
not the angry Black woman
society would love to label me.
Strong!

In love with
the divine feminine
energy that I bring.
I am me,
and she is I,
loving every part of my existence.

*Writing Prompt: **What have you discovered about yourself?***

_____

_____

_____

_____

_____

_____

_____

_____

_____

_____

_____

_____

_____

_____

_____

_____

_____

_____

_____

_____

_____

_____

_____

_____

_____

_____

_____

_____

_____

I Love You, Girl

I love you, girl.
Every freckle on your face,
Every dark mark
You hide with concealer,
Because those are the scars
That you hate.
You laid that foundation
Down
Effortlessly,
But I know it took
Hard work and dedication
To smile behind the face
That you painted to
Confuse the enemy.
Even though you look pretty on the outside,
It's the inside
That I know is tinted.

Future generations to come,
I raise my eyebrow,
Because they have no idea
What you had to grow through
To finally make it:
Prosecution and humiliation.
They laugh at the sight of your
Artistic flow,
But have the nerve to
Participate in copying your glow.

Throw that bronzer on, girl,
And structure your face!
That's the highlight of
What you show.
It's what they truly face.

Writing Prompt: What are you most ashamed of?

_____

_____

_____

_____

_____

_____

_____

_____

_____

_____

_____

_____

_____

_____

_____

_____

_____

_____

_____

_____

_____

_____

_____

_____

_____

_____

_____

_____

Love Unmatched

Have you ever
Met a love
So warm and gentle,
But like a father?
Protective
And gives correction?
Sweeps through
All your trials
And circumstances
As the answer?
Providing you with wisdom and insight,
Discerning all your worries
And issues?

In your mind, you fight
At night,
Waiting on you
To trust a love
You can cast your cares upon.
It'll cease
All your tears,
Direct your path
And allow you
The opportunity to face fears
You didn't know you had.
Seeing strength in you
That will have you to
Arrive at a place you have never
Elevated love.

Writing Prompt: When did you discover God's love?

_____

_____

_____

_____

_____

_____

_____

_____

_____

_____

_____

_____

_____

_____

_____

_____

_____

_____

_____

_____

_____

_____

_____

_____

_____

_____

_____

_____

_____

Promised Place

This is a place I've never been,
But yet promised
A place filled with love and laughter,
Milk and honey.
A divinely set
Table feast full
Of fruits and veggies.

Abundance awaits.
Our awake
Seems funny,
Seeing the unseen,
Hearing things
That make you wonder
In your beliefs.
As your fingertips grace the sand,
Watching the water separate from the land,
Quiet whispers of his voice,
Instructions are a choice,
Divinely aligned
With the truth that's inside.

Writing Prompt: Where is a place that you recently discovered is your safe place?

_____
_____
_____
_____
_____
_____
_____
_____
_____
_____
_____
_____
_____
_____
_____
_____
_____
_____
_____
_____
_____
_____
_____
_____
_____
_____

Relationship Building

Mama

Ma.
Mom.
Mommy.
You know I can't do this
Without you.
You gave me life.
It was your discussion
Of whether or not
You wanted to keep us.
And you did.
You raised us to be close.
You raised us to be strong.
You raised us to be uniquely ourselves.
Thanks for being the epitome of love.

Writing Prompt: What do you admire most about your mother?

_____

_____

_____

_____

_____

_____

_____

_____

_____

_____

_____

_____

_____

_____

_____

_____

_____

_____

_____

_____

_____

_____

_____

_____

Black Men

You grew up in neighborhoods
Where other young
Black brothers
Had to raise you.
Your mother did it
All alone.
Daddy wasn't there,
So you had to
Trust God
As your savior.
Drinking and
Drugging.
Days without it
Were unheard of.
Loud music playing
Conveniently enough
To hide the sound
Of the bullets
Shooting,
Sirens coming,
Everybody running.
Marijuana smoke in the air
Polluting;
Ball playing,
Hollering at girls
With the small waist
And the thick thighs;
Nobody told you
Saving yourself

Was cool;
It was how many t-shirts
And short skirts
You could pull.
Now I see you again
In the Potter's hands.
Reformed,
Something like new,
Who
You were intended to be
From the beginning.
Making your footsteps matter
In this country
That we live in,
Speaking your mind
So loud
And clear
Your voice echos
For generations
And generations
As they appear.
I see you,
Black man.
Educated,
Talented,
And tough.
Well rounded
With a sense of humor.
Adding pressure
And not letting up.
Family
Is what keeps
You grounded.

Single father,
No one sees the scars
You hide on your back
And your restless nights.
See,
No one wants to talk about
What our
Black men go through.
King,
I see you
Working hard
To make ends meet.
I hear you, King.
Even those words you don't speak.
I'm inspired,
As a Black queen,
To make sure
You're fed
Naturally,
As well as spiritually.
Feeding your brain
So you'll know
It's okay
Be vulnerable
And seek wise counsel.
Rub your back
And have random
Paid vacations
So you can relax.
You deserve that.
The wounds you bare
Are real.
Your strength,

Your courage
In today's society,
Is rare.
Everyone is giving up
On you,
But you
My Black kings
Refuse to fail.
You're worthy of
Accolades,
Praise,
And titles by your name.
I honor you today, King,
And always will.
Keep being the example
Our Black sons and daughters
Need to see.
I believe,
You believe,
Our Black men
Can be
Healed as kings.

Writing Prompt: What male in your life has inspired you?

_____

_____

_____

_____

_____

_____

_____

_____

_____

_____

_____

_____

_____

_____

_____

_____

_____

_____

_____

_____

_____

_____

_____

_____

_____

_____

_____

_____

Concrete Flower

Look at you!
Oh, how
You have grown.
Talking about your values, morals, and beliefs,
Standing strong.
You're a warrior,
Young man!
I know who you are.
Jumping out of planes,
Driving fast cars,
The love of history
And following Biblical principles
Are a few of your favorite
Pastimes.
Having private schools
Bringing awareness to the churches
That it could be a slavery concept.
If you don't know truth or purpose,
Indulge in the news.
Political views
Are just a few things
That you are
And dreaming to be.
You haven't even touched the surface of
The things you've imagined
You'll do
And the places
You'll see.
I know who you are.

You're driven by family love and self-control.
You took time to yourself.
Found out
You know more
About yourself
Than anyone else.
I know who you are.
You're an Alpha man.
Take pride in providing
For your family.
You have a heart of gold
And can talk to anyone,
Young or old.
You're funny, wild, and free.
A devoted father
And such a good friend to me.
I celebrate you today and every day.

Writing Prompt: Have you given flowers to a great male role model? If so, how so? How often?

_____

_____

_____

_____

_____

_____

_____

_____

_____

_____

_____

_____

_____

_____

_____

_____

_____

_____

_____

_____

_____

_____

_____

_____

_____

_____

_____

_____

_____

Confessions

You want to protect me
With your stature
When I need you to protect me
With your words.

My love language is affirmation,
So I'm quick to listen and slow to speak,
So I can hear what was said
And repeat to you what I heard.

I remember the moment
When I realized
I loved you.
I didn't know for sure
If you remember yours too,
But you show it
And take it back
Like you're tooling around with your soul
Which draws me to a place
Of abandonment.
Fear then takes control.

I have no idea
How we got to this place,
But it's scary as hell to me.
Please rescue me
From my thoughts
And just give my heart
What it needs.

Affirmation

Affection

Applauding, please.

I've prayed for firm love,
Not one
That's in between.
I need the reassurance
Kind of love,
The one that believes
Even the unseen.

No matter what lies in the future,
You just know
In your heart
As long as it's with me,
You're complete.

I want to be your person
And I know you want to be mine.
Let's stop fighting with our flesh.
Agree in the spirit
What we know in our minds.

Writing Prompt: What is your love language? What has it taught you about the way you desired to be loved?

_____

_____

_____

_____

_____

_____

_____

_____

_____

_____

_____

_____

_____

_____

_____

_____

_____

_____

_____

_____

_____

_____

_____

_____

_____

_____

_____

_____

Phases

I truly love you.
It is really crazy.
I never would imagine
Being here
In this place
Where we escape the world
And go off into the moon
And stars.

Eyes closed or open,
That's where you are,
Shining bright in my lenses.
Thoughts of you gives me
A clearer vision.

We were just kids
Skipping school,
Partying and drinking.
Memories after memories.
Laughter so loud.
We be trippin',
But honestly
That was our beginning.
Never no bad vibes.
Always greeted each other
With a hug and a kiss on the forehead
And when it's time to say goodbye.

But never in my eyes
I see the things I do today.
You pour into my emptiness,
Research my mind,
And supply me with the high energy
I need,
And give me what I deserve.
Honor me as a queen.
You do tell me about myself.
Sometimes it works my nerves,
But all these things
Are reasons why I love you,
Reasons why I care,
Reasons why you call me at three in the morning
Needing me.
I'll be there.

As long as I've known you,
You've always been around.
Even when you were gone
Serving our country,
We always found ways to talk.
We've had arguments
That led me
To want to walk away
From our friendship.
Even in those dark places
When we were apart,
Our souls were still connected
And you always remained in my heart.
Some kind of way,
You worked your way
Back into my life.

This time
It's different.
It's like we've been here before.
Now here we are again,
Revisiting.
My heart pounds,
Not knowing
What the outcome would be,
But I'm here
Sacrificing my fears
Just to see.

Writing Prompt: Describe a strong connection you felt with someone in different phases of your life.

_____

_____

_____

_____

_____

_____

_____

_____

_____

_____

_____

_____

_____

_____

_____

_____

_____

_____

_____

_____

_____

_____

_____

_____

_____

_____

_____

_____

_____

Atmosphere

So, I usually set the tone
And create an atmosphere
That's open
And warm enough
To acknowledge love's
Presence.
But when I saw you,
I just went in for the root.
No crying about
All the layers of betrayal
That bubbled up
To the surface.
I'm trying figure out
If we're on the same page,
Or how we got to this place
That feels so broken.
I was nervous for the response,
But my heart
Felt the need to get a remark,
Now sitting in regret
Cause you blew up
Like I thought you would.
Now, I'm in my head.
I'm in my own way.
I know what to do from now on:
Create an atmosphere
Where my peace
Can be found,
And I'll humbly
Fix my crown.

Writing Prompt: What does it look like when you're out of your comfort zone and you must create a safe environment?

_____

_____

_____

_____

_____

_____

_____

_____

_____

_____

_____

_____

_____

_____

_____

_____

_____

_____

_____

_____

_____

_____

_____

_____

_____

_____

Dear God

I think I know what I want now.

I want a love so fearless
It will shout out
Among any crowd.

A love so calm
It'll make peace
Sing as if
It's a song.

When my mind is raging
And waves are overtaking me,
It'll come right behind me,
Recusing me
With all bravery.

A love so real,
When it hurts
I feel.

Disappointments and discouragements,
They come and
They'll go,
But a love so strong,
Even when we are upset
We still won't let go.

I want a love so warm,
It puts me to bed at night.

Arguments turn to pillow fights.
A put the kids to sleep;
Let's get a quickie
And grab something to eat
Kind of love.

The one that work your nerves,
But sad when it's mad.
I want a love that is spiritually equipped
To fight battles
That come with
A purposeful relationship.

I want a love that can read my mind
And finish my sentences.

Know when I need a hug
And know when I need distance.
Balance between the two.

A love so indestructible
That'll it'll go pass the universe
And beyond any sea.

When I close my eyes,
It's almost like
I can feel it next to me.

Writing Prompt: Write out your desires to God.

_____

_____

_____

_____

_____

_____

_____

_____

_____

_____

_____

_____

_____

_____

_____

_____

_____

_____

_____

_____

_____

_____

_____

_____

_____

_____

_____

_____

_____

_____

Relationship
Lamentations

I Choose You

People would probably be surprised
When I say this,
But you're difficult
To love.

It was then
When I knew
I loved you
Because your imperfections
Drew me in
Like it
Knew me.

And then
I thought to myself
The Holy Ghost was right:
Our insecurities are alike,
But somehow different.
Your brokenness
Was the puzzle piece.
My picture
Was missing.

You inspire me,
Even in your constructive criticism.
Your decision-making
Is sometimes different.
But I love
When you make them

Because I get to listen
And you get to explain.

When we're together,
It's like we are kids
Playing on the playground.
It's like we're flying
And we're so free.
No one is around.
Just you and me.

It's hard to explain,
And sometimes
My feelings are strange.
Could something like this be real
Or is it
Just me
In my mind,
Creating a fantasy
Of unfolded stories
That
Has
Yet
Been revealed?

Either way,
I choose you
In my mind, in my heart, in my soul.
I'm sure you're the one
My heart prayed for,
And the one who will help
Restore
My soul.

Writing Prompt: Have you ever chosen to trauma bond with someone? Why or why not?

_____

_____

_____

_____

_____

_____

_____

_____

_____

_____

_____

_____

_____

_____

_____

_____

_____

_____

_____

_____

_____

_____

_____

_____

_____

_____

_____

_____

_____

_____

Feel

How you think he feels
When you're away?
Probably numbing the pain
In his mind,
Trying to justify
What he did.
Can't see the wrong
In what he do,
Because his ego
And insecurities
Won't allow him to.

Writing Prompt: How do you deal with your spouse or significant other's insecurities?

_____

_____

_____

_____

_____

_____

_____

_____

_____

_____

_____

_____

_____

_____

_____

_____

_____

_____

_____

_____

_____

_____

_____

_____

_____

_____

_____

Beautiful Lies

Beautiful lies,
They told you
To hold onto
The promises
They failed
To provide for you.

The restrictions are hell
Trying to move forward,
But all you can think about
Are all the good times
You had:

Smiling

Believing

All the lies they tell.

Holding you captive,
It's hard to escape
When, in your mind,
You've fallen for their potential.
Knowing every decision they make,
They forgot to mention
The importance
You hold in their life.
But let something go on in your world,
You don't think twice.
Sharing everything

In sight
God blessed you with.

Focus, girl.
You know their ways
Are not always right.
Stop giving your all
To people
That were only
Supposed to be a season in your life.

Writing prompt: What did you learn about yourself when you were around seasonal people?

_____
_____
_____
_____
_____
_____
_____
_____
_____
_____
_____
_____
_____
_____
_____
_____
_____
_____
_____
_____
_____
_____
_____
_____
_____
_____
_____
_____
_____
_____
_____

Residue

Is it the residue
that's still on you?
Screaming, lying, cheating, no good man.
Or is it a figment of my imagination,
playing tricks on my mind?
How do I know
when you abuse
your narcissistic personality?
Every other day,
you are so loving
when you are not
playing victim
instead of taking accountability.
It's too much like right.
As an alternative,
you fuss and scream
As if I wanted to fight.
All I did was express my feelings.
Now, I'm left alone
in my abandonment issues.
All these things you know.
It's tormenting every fiber,
every tissue.
But a part of me
Is at peace
being alone
because I've mastered
Being unchaperoned.
I've made it comfortable here

because the people
I loved
left me,
Which numbed me.
So now I've mastered
being alone
without any fear.
Or is the argument
all in my head,
tormented by past traumas.
ex-boyfriends,
and regrets?
That has me thinking things
I can't forget.
So, when I express myself,
I do it out of passion.
I'm not trying to accuse you.
My heart just needs to hear
what happened.
It needs reassurance often.
Am I asking for too much,
or should I give my insecurities
a nudge,
and tell them to quiet down?
That's enough.
Either way, I believe
the right one
would fight for me.
Thank you for a good time,
and for making my first lesson
about history.

Writing Prompt: Have you ever been in a relationship so long you started to see the changes you need to make within yourself? What were they?

_____
_____
_____
_____
_____
_____
_____
_____
_____
_____
_____
_____
_____
_____
_____
_____
_____
_____
_____
_____
_____
_____
_____
_____
_____

I Fell in Love with a Man

I fell in love with a man
Who didn't want to be loved
Or do anything in his power.

To give up?
I don't know what to do.
I gave you the purest parts
Of me.
All you did
Is project your insecurities
And carry my feelings
Carelessly.

I forgive you,
Honestly.
Because in order
To love you,
I have to love me.

Let go of
The shame, guilt, and trauma
From the past
Because I have
I see you.
I hear you.

The heart that
God made for you
Is beautiful.
Embrace it
Because you deserve
The love that God
Has for you, too.

Writing Prompt: Have you ever fallen for 'potential' or a 'representative'? What happened?

_____

_____

_____

_____

_____

_____

_____

_____

_____

_____

_____

_____

_____

_____

_____

_____

_____

_____

_____

_____

_____

_____

_____

_____

_____

_____

Matters of the Heart

I'm hurt,
Frustrated,
Aggravated and intimidated
All at the same time.
I can't hide
These feelings I feel.
They burst out the seams.
They're so real.
I tried to iron them with perfection,
But if you
Look close enough,
There are still wrinkles.
There's no neglecting.
I'm tired of crying over spilled milk.
I want to drink
From that desired cup that was spilled.
Patience is a virtue,
But what do you do
When your triggers pop up
And they want attention, too?
Bottle them up and push them down.
Tell my triggers
I know it's an indication
That my desires are not met,
But it's not the time to cry
About them yet.
I've done that for

Far too long.
All I have is God,
This paper,
This pen.
That's the only hope I have in this world
Of lies, betrayal, and sin.

Writing Prompt: List some of your triggers.

_____

_____

_____

_____

_____

_____

_____

_____

_____

_____

_____

_____

_____

_____

_____

_____

_____

_____

_____

_____

_____

_____

_____

_____

_____

_____

_____

Alone

I don't care anymore.
Some days I'm good,
And other days
I could care less
About the insecurities
You placed on me
Because you're not at your best.
All puffed up,
Projecting your stuff,
Playing the blame game.
My best bet is me.
Even alone,
I'll secure my emotional and mental stability.

Writing Prompt: Would you rather be alone or deal with someone's toxicity?

Prayer

Are you prepared
For what you're praying for,
Or are you just that scorned?
Love with condition
Is how you were conditioned,
Recognizing you needed a need
That, to a certain capacity,
The generation before us
Failed to meet.
Now you're empty inside,
Running around trying to fill a void,
But instead, you just end up
Self-sabotaging
And destroying the very
Thing you've been praying for.
Dealing with that consequence
Is a battle in itself.
You're fighting the solution
To your problem,
Playing the villain,
Crying desperately for help
When you're at fault.
You got what you needed.
Maybe not what you wanted,
But what you deserved.

Praying

Asking

Believing for something
You couldn't maintain
Or control.
No one at fault
But you
And your conditions.
Selfish ways
Got you here.
Now repent
And ask God for forgiveness
For praying for things
You weren't ready for.
Prepare yourself for the blessings
You're asking for
So, when it comes
You won't be blinded
By the cloudiness
Of your past experiences.
Then, and only then, will you be able
To recognize an answered prayer
When it's in your presence,
And not bruise it
Alongside a road
Somewhere where you left it.

Writing Prompt: Describe a time when you mishandled something or someone whom you believe was sent from God.

_____

_____

_____

_____

_____

_____

_____

_____

_____

_____

_____

_____

_____

_____

_____

_____

_____

_____

_____

_____

_____

_____

_____

_____

_____

Encouragement

God's Creation

As I look at the sea,
I think
That is the same God
That created me.
Why am I
Losing sight
Of my identity?
He is the one
Who created the universe,
And said it was good.
Why do I
Feel guilty
About how
Someone else feels
About me?
What's understood
Doesn't have to be explained.
My God acts up
When you say some
Foul stuff
And mention my name.
I'm the one
He doesn't play about.
Be careful.
I know
To you, it's just words,
But to my God,
It's the slander
That hurts.

The misinterpretation,
The reckless behaviors.
You're not going to treat
His daughter any kind of way
And believe you will have
His favor.
He doesn't work like that.
And it is sad that you would
Think He would
Deal with someone else
On an entry-level.
My creator
Tapped me on my shoulder
And reminded me
I'm good.

Writing Prompt: What are three things you have fully accepted about yourself?

_____

_____

_____

_____

_____

_____

_____

_____

_____

_____

_____

_____

_____

_____

_____

_____

_____

_____

_____

_____

_____

_____

_____

_____

_____

_____

I Cried Today

I cried today.

Only this time,
It was tears of joy.

My mind, body, soul
Escaped my current reality,
Pushed me past my past,
Glanced at my now
And woke up to my future.

It's bright,
It's shiny,
It's what I've imagined
Plus more.

Every vibration of my being
Has me believing.
Taking care of the things today
Means achieving little by little,
Step by step.
Accomplished things
Will always be my tomorrow.

Slow and steady
Wins the race
So I closed the noise
Of others' expectations
Of me
And maneuver at my own pace,

Enjoying the journey
As I arrive at my destination:
Close family and friends.
Of course, my love for God
Will always be my motivation.

Faith has me traveling, modeling, being an entrepreneur
And aspiring others in different locations.
Breaking grounds
My ancestors couldn't,
Breaking generational curses
Others before me
Wouldn't.
Building generational wealth.
Growing and glowing,
Shedding off the stinking thinking
And living the currently positively positive,
Knowing what I know.

Believing in the things I can't see,
Achieving endless possibilities,
Are my joys.
No more sorrows.
I can do all things
Through Christ that
Strengthens me.
The enemy knows that.
That's why he is scorned.
I just realized
It's my purpose
To confuse the enemy.
That's why I was born.

*Writing Prompt: **What are you most proud of?***

_____

_____

_____

_____

_____

_____

_____

_____

_____

_____

_____

_____

_____

_____

_____

_____

_____

_____

_____

_____

_____

_____

_____

_____

_____

_____

Blessing and Curse

I thank God
For the blessings
And curses.
It all has
To happen.

Get the lesson
That is learned,
Then
Figure out
What awaits after.
I'm sure it's full
With more
Life lessons.

Bleeding
From scars
That'll eventually
Heal
Following
A blessing
That makes
You question
Whether the
Trial
Is real,
Or is it something

God is trying to show
You
To make your vision
From blurry to
Clear.

Writing Prompt: List some things that literally tried to destroy you, but they made you more than a conqueror.

_____

_____

_____

_____

_____

_____

_____

_____

_____

_____

_____

_____

_____

_____

_____

_____

_____

_____

_____

_____

_____

_____

_____

_____

Tomorrow's Trust

Trust tomorrows
Because they give
You what you need to
Look ahead.
When the dark days
Are cloudy
And you're full of rage,
Understand it's just
A moment of disappointment
Wrapped up
In distractions.
I promise you
You're safe.
Life has a funny way
Of showing you
What you're
Supposed to be doing.
Get to doing it.
Life will drown you
In misery
When you don't
Address your pain
And when you don't
Follow your dreams.
So quit trying to escape.
Aren't you tired of explaining
Yourself
To the same people
Who are not
Going in your direction,

Or dare offer any kind of help?
I know you felt
Those different personalities
Drive you insane.
Focus on the direction
God called you to
So, your purpose
On this earth
Won't be in vain.

Writing Prompt: What disappointments did you have to overcome?

_____

_____

_____

_____

_____

_____

_____

_____

_____

_____

_____

_____

_____

_____

_____

_____

_____

_____

_____

_____

_____

_____

_____

_____

_____

_____

_____

Thank You

Dear God,
Thank You
For hearing everything
I said in
The letter I wrote
In the journal
Kept by the bed.
You opened my eyes
Even the more,
Allowing me to know
Everything
I endured
Was preparation for my now,
Giving me the keys to the doors
Only faith restored.
I'm grateful
For my Adam,
The one I can call my own.
I finally get to experience
Perfect love
That casts out all fear.
You gave me something
Rare, but real.
I'm his rib,
And he knows it, too.
God,
I see Your hand
All in the midst.
I feel Your glory

All over this.
With every conversation,
Even unspoken things
That we have missed,
I'm appreciative
Father,
For the answered prayers
And every tear
You stored in a battle for me.
Not only did
You grant my desires,
But you gave me exactly
What I need.

Writing prompt: How do you demonstrate your gratitude to God?

_____

_____

_____

_____

_____

_____

_____

_____

_____

_____

_____

_____

_____

_____

_____

_____

_____

_____

_____

_____

_____

_____

_____

_____

_____

_____

About the Author

Hello!

Let me introduce myself. My name is Shakira Henderson, a girl from the small town of Salisbury who was raised in a house with both of her parents and four brothers. I am a mother, a business owner, and now an author.

Just like I birthed this book out of grapple, I birthed my daycare business out of the same desperation. God aligned me to His will and pushed me out my comfort zone to walk in faith. My daughter, who suffers from an intellectual delay disability, was forced to be home due to the Pandemic, but because I was a childcare worker, I was labeled essential and had to punch that clock every day. My daughter struggled to log into class. Her difficulty gave me anxiety, which resulted in me sacrificing my job and becoming an entrepreneur.

I had been in childcare for fifteen years before I started my own home daycare business. Looking back, it was the best decision I ever made. It brings me great joy to be able to service the families in my community.

Since I was young girl, I always knew I would work in education. My Aunt Roxie was a teacher, and when I was young, she would take me to the school each year to help her break down her classrooms for the summer. Before the school year began again I would help with bulletin boards and the decorations for the classroom. That was the sparkle that burst the flame.

I took Career and Technical Education throughout high school, which gave me my credentials upon graduating. I've worked in some of the best daycares on the eastern shore and gained a lot of knowledge and wisdom during those times.

My greatest accomplishment is succeeding past all the titles that were given to me as a child—intellectually delayed, dyslexic, illiterate and slow—and giving you this book.. When people say if I can do it, so can you, believe me when I say it's the God-honest truth.

This is why I call myself the Misfit Author. What was meant for evil God turned for good.

- Genesis 50:20

www.ingramcontent.com/pod-product-compliance
Lightning Source LLC
Chambersburg PA
CBHW060341130626
46553CB00003B/1075